SURVIVING THE APOCALYPTIC SOCIETY

A DECLARATIVE VOICE THAT COMES FROM WITHIN

MOHMOD IRFAN SHAH

Copyright © Mohmod Irfan Shah
All Rights Reserved.

This book has been published with all efforts taken to make the material error-free after the consent of the author. However, the author and the publisher do not assume and hereby disclaim any liability to any party for any loss, damage, or disruption caused by errors or omissions, whether such errors or omissions result from negligence, accident, or any other cause.

While every effort has been made to avoid any mistake or omission, this publication is being sold on the condition and understanding that neither the author nor the publishers or printers would be liable in any manner to any person by reason of any mistake or omission in this publication or for any action taken or omitted to be taken or advice rendered or accepted on the basis of this work. For any defect in printing or binding the publishers will be liable only to replace the defective copy by another copy of this work then available.

Contents

Publishing-in-support

Publishing-in-support-of,

sarafali.in
The voice of unpublished writings.

Mohalla Sultanpura, opp partap exclusive hostel Wali Gali, main stop Janipur, Jammu - 180007

Facebook: sarafbhat | sarafali101@gmail.com

The opinions/ contents expressed in this book are solely of the author and do not represent the opinions/ standings/ thoughts of sarafali.in

Preface

This book presents a sophisticated response to the question of what constitutes social problems and mental health deterioration, with thirteen entries giving a range of perspectives on the central problem issues of our generation. It also includes the author's personal experience and how he managed his stressed life in today's society. It also provides valuable suggestions for social issues and mental health. The topics cover areas of concern connected with physical and mental health, poverty, education, violence and crime, family and social relationships, etc. Every age group from different backgrounds will find this book helpful, whether casual readers or students.

The author's experiences with dating, breakups, literary life, therapists, the world, the arts, family, and social media are all explored in this book. The author's keen perceptions of the human experience and brilliant clarity give us a vision of what the current generation is going through, physically, virtually, verbally, socially or mentally.

Acknowledgements

Firstly, I am grateful to my parents, teachers and friends who have always supported me.

*Writing a book is more complicated and rewarding than I could have imagined. But, without my friend **Saraf Ali**, none of this would have been possible. He was the first friend I made, when I moved to SSM College of Engineering, who helped me bring this book into the public domain.*

*Most importantly, I am grateful to **Mahyah Binti Idris**.*

In my life, many people offered support, but few have put their words into action, and I can't express how much her support helped me with this book and my writing career.

*I am highly grateful to **Irtiza Khurshid**, who is my teacher. She has always been the person I could turn to during those dark and desperate years. She sustained me in ways that I never knew that I needed.*

About The Author

Mohmod Irfan Shah is a student pursuing B.E Civil Engineering from SSM College of Engineering, parihaspora pattan. He has been fond of writing since childhood. He is a Columnist, poet and co-author of three anthologies.

After more than one year of penning articles for the local daily newspapers of Jammu and Kashmir, Mohmod Irfan Shah has acquired a particularly declarative voice that comes through his most recent collection of articles exploring social and mental trauma in today's era.

CHAPTER ONE

Causes, Contribution and Overcoming Self-Harm

"Believe in yourself that you can overcome any period of your life with all these simple tips; Set your goals, don't let your emotions control who you are, choose everything wisely, stay calm and focus on yourself.

Mohmod Irfan Shah"

Cutting, injuring, harming, or scratching oneself deliberately is a major issue that influences the youth of the 21st century. Like other concerns of life, cutting can be perilous and habitual. In the majority of the cases, it is an indication of sorrow or deep misery. This negative behaviour pattern found in today's generation is because of a plurality of factors such as loneliness, loss of a loved one, being a victim of abuse, school or college pressure, arguments or problems with friends or classmates, mental health issues, difficulties at home, peer pressure, and much more. It can even be considered a common act of some personality disorders.

Self-harm can be non-suicidal, but it is life-threatening because we never know how deep the person will cut him/herself, how lethal the intake of drugs is; so self-harm is not less than a suicide attempt. Self-harm can increase the chances of suicide for the individual because of more pressure, ignorance by people around, and overburdening emotional pain.

Blades, needles, scissors, knife or any pointed metallic objects are being used by victims of self-harm as a tool to scratch or cut themselves. Believe me, it is a belief in most of the people around us that self-harming is an attention-seeking behaviour, but it is incorrect in the majority of the cases as most of the self-harmers are conscious of their injuries, cuts, and scars, which makes them feel guilty for what they are doing.

Suicide is forbidden under Islamic law, according to evidence from the Qur'an, Sunnah, and Muslim scholars. The Qur'an reiterates believers to trust the Almighty, have faith in His mercy, have patience, and not to destroy one's own life.

"Nor kill (or destroy) yourselves: for verily Allah hath been to you Most Merciful!" The Qur'an, An-Nisa (4:29)

What can be the cause of self-harm?

We cannot paint everyone with the same brush; hence a general reason cannot be quoted as to why people harm themselves. There can be different reasons for different individuals; it may be because of a lack of understanding or communication. Some may think that it is the only way to relieve anxiety and depression. Such people try to overcome their mental pain by physically hurting themselves, making them feel numb, the pain that makes them feel suicidal, and the pain that they feel is unbearable emotionally. Any recent traumatic experience, bullying, breakup, sexual assault, or feeling that one cannot take all the sadness anymore can be considered among the prime reasons that push people to harm themselves physically. They may have difficulty being social or sharing their emotions with people around, or they may feel lonely even amidst a crowd; the feeling of being separated is what makes them hurt themselves. There may be a history of self-harming, which becomes an addiction later on.

Self-hatred can also be one reason for self-harming. The victim might develop hate for him/ herself for being different than other people, underestimating themselves for not being capable of doing things like other people, or feeling uglier than other people.

How can we at a personal level help such people?

In the first place, we have to stop shaming, blaming, making people in our day-to-day lives feel guilty for the small mistakes they make because we never know what one might be going through emotionally. Try to socialize with people, listen to them, and understand what they are going through instead of making fun of other peoples' emotions. Being a secret listener without sharing their personal issues in public will make them feel better. If self-harming has become an addiction for them, take them to a psychiatrist or a professional person who has gone through the same, who can really help them. We can encourage them by reminding them of their capabilities and responsibilities, which might make them feel responsible and capable of being alive. Make them busy by indulging in productive activities like learning a new language, cooking, baking, crocheting or any stuff that they like more, or what their hobby is or take them out of the station where they can forget all their worries or a place where they feel they are equally important, like volunteering activities.

If you find anyone talking about self-harm or they have attempted to kill themselves, do not take it lightly. Try to approach that person personally and try to offer the best kind of help.

How did I overcome the habit of self-harming?

Years ago, when I was in higher secondary school, I had become habitual to self-harm. It had become a habit to harm myself physically after every emotional pain. The main reason for my scars used to be social networking sites, where I found people hurting themselves in different ways to get over emotional traumas. The more emotional pain I had, the more physical pain I gave to myself to become numb and cancel out the pain. Fighting with friends, colleagues, parents, or loneliness used to terrify me and make me hurt myself more. Eventually, all these scars drifted me to end my life in 2019; I couldn't resist the sudden feeling of being away from home and the college pressure. I consumed a handful of medicines to end my life. It was a near-death experience. I woke up after 24 hours, and I couldn't believe I was alive after eating a handful of medicines. It was all because my friends rushed me to the hospital, where doctors washed my stomach. I got gifted with a new life when I felt that I woke up, and it was then I realized what actually should matter and whatnot. This incident taught me that life is full of happiness, which we usually deny. After the incident, everyone began to point at my character, the ones who didn't even know me started alleging me with baseless labels, which made my vision clearer; it taught me who really loves me and who is just showing their fake love. Things turned well after this incident, and I came to realize that sorrows are not the end of life. After coming over anxiety, depression, and pain, I realized these are just the part of life that gives you some opportunities to change your life, giving you ample time to think about what is going wrong and how to fix it.

Believe in yourself that you can overcome any period of your life with all these simple tips; Set your goals, don't let your emotions control who you are, choose everything wisely, stay calm and focus on yourself, and most importantly, listen to what people have to say but, don't let people interfere in your decisions and most importantly stay in the company of motivating people, people who make you realise your importance, listen and understand your needs.

There is a specific day for self-harm Awareness on March 1, but instead of creating awareness on one day, as an individual, we should help our friends as well as our close ones every time. It's important to understand that we won't always feel the way we do today. Remember that change is the only constant, and the difficulties that are leading people to self-harm can, with assistance and support, become more bearable over time and go away. Things can and can get better.

CHAPTER TWO

Social Media: An Obscured Disaster?

We are in that age of information technologies where we have self-driving cars, 3-D Printers, Space Exploration, Social Media, Bluetooth, fiber optics, and much more. This technology has proven to change our lives for the better by providing us with several advantages, including unlimited communication, saving our time, treating incurable diseases, easy ways to earn money, easy traveling, and much more. But social media, being one of the most used technology by all age groups, is becoming menacing at an alarming rate, negatively impacting our lives.

Social media, one of the fundamental modern technology, is becoming a reason for Psychological and physical issues, less sleep, and time-wasting resources. People of all age groups are addicted to smartphones at a higher rate, be it a newborn baby who doesn't eat without watching cartoons/YouTube, teens who have isolated themselves from their family and friends, or retired employees who find it hard to sleep without scrolling on their phones. Smartphones were invented for easy and accessible communication, keeping people updated with this technological world, or doing/watching our important tasks on small screens instead of large computers/ televisions. But unfortunately, they are not being used appropriately, which in turn is negatively impacting our lives.

As reported by Pew Research Center, 97 percent of 13- to 17-year-olds use at least one of seven major online platforms, and the average teen ages 13 to 18 spends about nine hours on social media each day; tweens ages 8 to 12 are on for about six hours a day.

In the following paragraphs, I have discussed some severe drawbacks that social media has on our mental as well as physical health:

1. Self-Isolation:-

A majority of people from all age groups prefer sitting alone while surfing social media. Either they don't want others to notice them or are afraid of being caught while watching explicit content which pops up on every social media site. Social media is becoming a reason for people being antisocial or people not wanting to face anyone physically. People are turning into introverts as they are not much into physical talks anymore. Social media is pushing people to build virtual relationships, which expels them from the physical world. Self-Isolation eventually leads to anxiety, distress, and suicidal thoughts.

2. Lower Self-Estcem:-

People have started underestimating themselves while following the lifestyle of so-called "influencers" on different online platforms. They portray themselves like top celebrities, social media influencers, and models, which builds an inferiority complex. They blame themselves for not being capable of doing things that other people post about themselves, which makes them forget about their capabilities, exclusiveness, and specialty. Stalking the life of other people on social media makes them feel as if they are unprivileged and that everyone else on the internet is living their best life. Most of us forget that social media is an illusion and that people only post the positive side of their life on social media. Nobody would post the flaws or problems of their life, and we often ignore this truth.

3. Cyber-Bullying:-

Cyber-Bullying is the harassment or bullying done over social media. It is so common in teenagers that you will find numerous cases of online bullying now and then. Cyber Bullying includes posting rumors, threats, sharing victim's personal information, spreading hatred about the victim or can be of any other form which disturbs the mental peace of an individual. Cyber bullying is one of the most distressing evil in our society, and its root cause is social media. I personally have been a victim of cyber bullying and at times have had nightmares as well as suicidal thoughts because of it. The bully makes fun of the victim in social groups or posts is a standard form of Cyber-Bullying, which is being taken as a source of humor by Cyber bystanders. According to StopBullying.org, The percentages of individuals who have experienced cyber bullying at some point in their lifetimes have more than doubled (18% to 37%) from 2007-2019.

4. Decreased Activity:-

Before we adopted the norm of being glued to our electronic gadgets, children were found playing with mud, families used to go for picnics with their relatives, or even neighbors during the summer, and old ones used to keep themselves busy by going through their religious books or counting their last breathe. Thus, the social interaction before we got addicted to social media was relatively high compared to what we get to witness now. Back then, parents used to force their children to come back home, but they didn't want to stop playing with their friends outside; on the contrary, these children are now sitting at their homes using smartphones, totally isolated from any social interaction. Today we see a lesser number of children in playfields. Children are busy playing online games or surfing social media, which harms their physical as well as mental health because of which they are exposed to bad posture, physical and psychological stress, eye strain, etc. Adults who used to be busy with office work and household chores are usually scrolling social media, leading to the same problem. Older people are being avoided, as every family member is busy scrolling, making them feel lonesome.

5. Suicide/Self-Harm/18+ Content:-

One of the significant concerns related to social media, which is harming a considerable number of people, is the kind of content that people follow, make or find on social media. The majority of the posts on social media have no age-restricted filter or warning for different age groups. To find explicit or suicidal content on the internet is just a search away. Images or video clips of self-harming or 18+ content have no warnings about graphic content. All this can develop an intimacy disorder or may cause trauma in the younger generation. Children copy most of the acts from social media, where they find Self-harming content, which later pushes them to imitate the same actions.

Hence, it becomes a moral responsibility for all of us, including me, to take our time off the internet as well as smartphones. Also, parents play a vital role in disciplining the younger generation; they have to educate their children about the good and the bad aspects of the internet. Parents should hold their children accountable if they witness any disturbing act their child commits if he/ she is too young for it. A weekly or monthly report about the child's behavior should be made for children by the teachers and submitted to their parents. On the other hand, adults should spend some time with their friends, family, and themselves and be grateful for their life and the privileges they have rather than comparing their life with people on the internet.

CHAPTER THREE

Is too much competition in the Education Sector Detrimental?

"Life is not known until you don't mark your destiny, so it is better to create your own path, follow your strategies, and reach your destination.

Mohmod Irfan Shah"

"Life is a race; if you don't run fast, you'll get trampled." this is one of the dialogues of the most famous movie of all the time, 3 Idiots, said by Viru Sahastrabudhhe AKA Virus (Boman Irani). Unfortunately, our society has taken the same sentence seriously. Taking life as a race means you got no time to rest, as the other person might overtake you and you will lose. Life is not known until you don't mark your destiny, so it is better to create your own path, follow your strategies, and reach your destination.

Life itself starts with a competition when society asks who you gave birth to - a boy or a girl? This is when society forgets that both chromosomes XX and XY are equally responsible for the population growth and continuity of the human race. Competition is somehow essential for the development and betterment of society, but it has made us so selfish that we forget about what we are competing with, why we are competing and what ways we are adopting to compete and eventually, competing is becoming disastrous for the mental health of our society.

Competition in the education sector of our society is on the crest. We notice that since day one of our crèche, till we complete our college/ university, we have to compete with students who are good at the syllabus prescribed by the school or college, forgetting about what we are good at. Indeed, education is the right of every child, but even if we are good at activities like painting, writing, playing, or technical stuff other than the academic course, we are not allowed to do that. Why? Because of the current scenario in our society that is pushing us in the wrong direction, we forget our passion and strength; in turn, we start competing in a field we never wanted to be part of. We face difficulties, failures and eventually degrade our mental health. It's not that what we want to pursue, but you may ask that if we follow what we dream of, will we reach the skies in the first go, without struggling or without difficulties? Of course not, we will indeed go through difficulties and have equal chances of failing, but that failure won't mean the end to us, because it will be our dream, passion, our goal, we won't stop till we don't achieve, and we will do everything happily to achieve it. What we usually notice is that parents force their children after 10th to take medical (PCB) or non-medical (PCM) or, in the worst cases, medical plus non-medical (PCBM) as their core subject even if they don't want to take it. It becomes a compulsion for children because everyone opts for it. Elders and parents emotionally torture their kids by using phrases like, "Hum toh tumharay ache kai liay he keh rahay hain" (We are saying this for your own good), "Agar unkay bachhe ne medical pakda tou tum mai konsi khaami hai?" (If so and so chose medical, what do you lack?) hence, they ask us to follow the herd. If someone gets good marks in science or mathematics in class 10, they are suggested to opt for medical, non-medical or both.

Passing matriculation is the first ruining point for students who have passed high school and want to do something different after that. But unfortunately, due to various factors, including pressure from parents and relatives, the child is forced to choose subjects in which they secured good marks in matriculation. The poor mental health of students is because of the social pressure. Every parent wants their child to be better than other children, wants his child to get a degree better than other children, i.e., a majority of parents try to experiment with their children's career. Parents forget that the child they have given birth to has grown into an individual and has their own dreams and goals. They fail to understand their children; this eventually leads to multiple failures in the child's career, which they never wanted to be a part of, resulting in depleting mental health. The serious misleading point in our society is clearing JEE/ NEET, getting a seat in a Government or leading private college for Medical or Engineering studies. After clearing their class 12th exams, students struggle in competitive exams; they drop year after year, desperately waiting to secure qualifying marks or the end of life, all because they see only two options in front of them, and this is all because of the pressure by society, parents, teachers, and your so-called "friends" competing against you. Did anyone ask that student what do you want to be? No! Society wants everyone to be Doctors and Engineers as if all other professions have no respect or income. Keeping Medicine and Engineering as the only two career options for your child is where you are misguiding them, the sapling you want to turn into a fruitful and shadow providing tree will wither away forever in any autumn season, where they will see no rain, no light, no season of spring and eventually fall off. Providing financial, physical, and emotional support to your child is a fundamental right of every child, but forcing decisions on your kids can be inutile. There can be no one better than parents to guide their children in choosing their career, but instead, we see parents pushing their children for a seat in Medical or Engineering College. We live in a society where teaching our children better than our neighbour has become a competition. How unfortunate is it that children are treated as pawns to checkmate our neighbours or relatives?

The decision making on choosing a career should be personal with some professional career counselling. Parents should talk with their children about the field they desire to pursue a professional career in. Parents should also evaluate their children and the potential that they possess. There should be a thorough discussion of all the advantages and disadvantages of pursuing a particular professional path. But, unfortunately, we lack such a system and believe in manufacturing doctors and engineers in private and government colleges with the societal pressure even if our child is good at other things. Decisions are made with the support of parents, teachers and elders but not by the one whose career is at stake. Every individual is their own best judge. One knows their capabilities and can accordingly pursue whatever he/ she wishes for. Our mantra for life should be: "Whatever it is that you like doing, turn it into a profession, and then labour will no longer appear to be work, but rather a joy." We must remember that career is not dependent on what you are pursuing or what grades you get, many success stories of great personalities like Stephen Hawking, Vincent Van Gogh, Walt Disney, Steven Spielberg, Michael Jordan, Abraham Lincoln, Albert Einstein, Bill Gates, Steve Jobs, J.K. Rowling and much more we cannot even count, are proof of this. Also, everyone says that once you qualify or achieve something, we will throw a party and celebrate, but no one says if you fail, we will be there for you. Are we forgetting that failure is a part of life and there always is a chance of failing? Why are we running towards perfection when we should just accept our failures as life lessons? The only problem with failing is that it takes a tremendous amount of work to get back up and convince yourself that you should keep going once you have fallen.

We judge a student's ability based on their grades. Lack of freedom for students to pursue their interests outside of the classroom is one of the main drawbacks of our education system. All students are forced to study the same courses and go through the same educational process, even though many of the things they are taught will be irrelevant a few years down the road. Of course, basic literacy is required, but forcing students to study the same topics for twelve years before choosing an area of study appears to be an ancient rule. There is a serious need for an education system that does not compel children to be showpieces of their efforts.

CHAPTER FOUR

Stress – Sabotaging College Students!

College life is difficult since they mark the beginning of individual, adult life. Initial days of college may be distressing for many students since it requires the initiation of a new friend circle, implementing new study habits relevant to the selected course, dealing with work overload, utilizing time effectively, and moving to rented rooms or college hostel. The same student has to face additional pressures, such as fear about finding a job after graduation. So far, research indicates that many students struggle to manage these stresses and that the prevalence of stress among students is rising. It has a negative impact on mental health, among other things.

College years are critical developmental years in student's life as they progress from teenage to adulthood. College students, particularly 1ˢᵗ-year students, confront a slew of difficulties in making the effective transition. Life pressures can worsen these difficulties, which differ amongst pupils based on objective situations and mental resistance. Although stress is a natural part and parcel of life and may even be motivating in specific cases, high amounts of stress are harmful to one's well-being and academic achievement.

Causes of Stress in College Students:

Some of you may support that college students do not face any sort of pressure. Because most of you believe that all a student needs to do is attend class, clear a few examinations, and graduate. But unfortunately, this is not the case. College students' suffer tremendous stress, affecting many aspects of their lives. Let me put forth some causes of stress in college students:

Academic Stress: Class prerequisites might be overwhelming. Most professors expect learners to complete homework on time, submit assignments on time, self-study and prepare for unexpected assessments. In addition, some ask students to present research articles and publications and enroll in extracurricular activities. When you add all of those activities together and increase them by four, five, or six more subjects, you can see how difficult it may be for college students. Managing time for Trainings, internships, Courses during college hours adds more to one's stressful life. However, not all academic stress is because of the lecturer. Some of it is due to poor time management and deadlines, while some are due to the pupils' parents or seniors.

Financial Stress:

Every student is worried about their financial situation. They are concerned about how they will pay for courses or tuitions they are opting for, repay loans, and pay for hostel and needs while breathing on a fixed income of their own. Even students whose parents pay the whole expenditure of their education are worried about money. Many students do not want to bother their parents for financial assistance during college life, but they are aware that they require financial assistance. As a result of feeling bad about spending their parents' resources, students seek extra financial help from Banks or go for part-time jobs, which in turn affect their studies. Some of them either quit their course for a year or two so that they can earn before they resume their course. Even some of them quit after a year or two for a class forth job, so that they be independent as soon as possible.

Job Outlook Stress:

Students should look for a job with a handsome salary that would allow them to pay off their loans as soon as possible. However, not all potential employment can offer this benefit. The realization that they will not be able to repay their loans for several years leads to stress. When students understand they must-have attributes that set them apart from the other job seekers, their stress level rises. These include doing additional work, volunteering, or participating in extracurricular activities. Job seeking, believe it or not, adds more stress to a student's life. With so many college graduates competing for the same entry-level position, students feel as though they want to quit to escape denials and rejections. Students may believe that academic accomplishment is one method to outperform their peers. As a result, they work hard academically to get the greatest grades and awards, which eventually leads to academic stress. After completing the degree, when most batch mates either get admission for higher studies or get a job, it adds to the distress of students who are still clearing their backlogs. Staying at home after the degree pushes such students to work as class 4th where their degree is not considered.

Social pressure: Students are frequently subjected to undue stress by parents, Relatives, and Friends Circle. Parents believe that by imposing high expectations on them, they assist them. However, it frequently leads to increased pressure. Families are not without imperfections. All of the flaws in your family might contribute to an overburden of tension. Divorce, family financial conditions, and poor communication are some of the challenges families encounter that can cause stress for kids. Many college students strive to satisfy their parents, even though their parents or guardians assure them that they are happy no matter what. It is an inherent urge to make the family proud and demonstrate that their money is not being misused. In most cases, parents give examples of neighbours and relatives to their kids, which their children take as a challenge and later, when they fail, they land up in depression.

Trying to manage due deadlines, assessments in college, sleep, health, and social and personal life, causes stress. Stress management may result in a better attitude, more productivity, and a better mindset. That's why students require a self-care strategy. Did you imagine that stress may cause illness? You can establish routes to release stress and avoid stress-related illnesses if you can properly cope with it.

For that, you can practice these simple tips:

Maintain a study routine: Stress can be more prevalent than usual during examination times. Make a timetable and follow it to aid with these moments of possible tension. Consider taking pauses for relaxation, exercise, and nutritious meals, and be sure to divide your study time evenly across your topics, focusing on those that require more assistance.

Do what makes you feel comfortable: When you don't want to do anything for others, learn to say "NO". When you're anxious, don't add another responsibility to your diary. It will increase your stress and may end in you disappointing someone. When you can't take much more, learn to say no.

It's easy for students to take on more than they can handle between academics, extracurricular activities, and sometimes even jobs. If you've signed up for too many classes, don't be afraid to abandon one. Start treating yourself the same as you would take care of your child.

Take special, loving attention to yourself.

Don't give up your passions: Your routine may be packed with classes, courses, seminars and workgroups, but try to set all your routine work aside at least once a week to pursue a hobby or other enjoyable activity. Do something that nourishes your heart's peacefulness and stay in touch with it; it creates anti-stress physiology in your brain. Don't let your academic life suppress your potential and capabilities if you are good at anything. Time belongs to you, so it wholly and solely depends on you how you give time to your course and your hobbies equally.

CHAPTER FIVE

Harassment- The Blood-Curdling Evil

""Our lives begin to end
The day we become silent
About things that matter."
-**Martin Luther King, Jr.**"*

Harassment is any behaviour that makes another person feel uneasy. It is possible to encounter it in both public and private spaces. Harassment of women is a global problem that affects women in every country. Sexual harassment is considered as the most prevalent form of harassment experienced by women, but there are more types of harassment faced by women which are being neglected, which includes psychological, sexual orientation, online, workplace, verbal, and even visual Harassment.

A majority of us might have heard about stories on various social media platforms or news outlets about the harassment of women, as well as young girls. But, I, at a personal level, wanted to know whether women I am acquainted with in real life, whether via college, social media platforms or blood relation, have faced harassment of any sort. And, to my surprise, the results disgusted me. I conducted an online survey via Google form, which was anonymous, within a target audience of around forty young girls from age 18 to 24, out of which a high percentage of respondents claimed that they have been harassed or eve-teased at least once in their life.

Below are the key take-away points from my short survey:

• There is no specific age group of Harassers; they belong from the tender age of 12 to the dotage of 70, or shockingly less or more than that.

• People around the victim didn't react most of the times, either they didn't notice, or they just didn't care as the victim who was being harassed didn't belong to their family or friend circle.

• The victim of the harassment preferred to stay quiet, fearing that the society might point their finger towards her character or blame her for the same or they were just worried about the family reputation.

• Harassers can be from your locality, friend circle, school, workplace, relatives, or anyone from the general public or even someone who nobody can ever doubt, judging based on looks.

• Harassment cases come from online gaming platforms, Social media platforms, public places, workplaces, or even homes.

The victims' silence is one of the main causes which gives the harasser the green signal. When a woman is the victim, she usually keeps her feelings to herself. In public buses or trains, she may leave or change her seat, and a very few object. Even if she does raise an alarm, the odds of her being rescued are slim. Women are raised to tolerate and accept the deep-seated patriarchy. Even the elderly seldom expect a change in their favour and presume the situation would remain unchanged. It is deplorable to be in a society where harassment and eve-teasing are common. Girls are generally pushed behind the veil, especially in rural regions. They are told to not speak about their concerns or opinions. The terrible reality of poverty makes them stay in the conditions of unease for the purpose of pleasing the community. Knowing the fact that the harasser is the one who needs to change his behaviour, his acts, his approach, we still stop victims from living their life. So many crimes are committed every day; does that mean we hide in our homes and stop living our lives thinking that we might become a target for someone too? No, right? The offender should be afraid, not the victim. Instead of punishing and stopping a harasser from doing such mischievous acts and educating our society about the right kind of behaviour, we control the victims of harassment by refraining them from wearing a dress of their choice, using social media platforms or going out alone with friends.

Women endure a huge amount of online harassment in the current scenario due to their gender identification. However, online abuse based on gender is not well recognised. Social media platforms and online gaming platforms are the major mediums for gender-based online harassment. The effect of such acts on women can be damaging to both their personal life and career.

Digital harassment limits women's capacity to participate in online activities like gaming, social media, or even online classes on equal ground with men. While women may be able to discuss their experiences in private forums online using Hashtags. Women who publicly oppose male social domination are constantly suppressed. But, I firmly believe that despite the pain that internet harassment causes, women have the capacity to defend themselves and their careers from unlawful persons.

Harassment has a substantial psychological as well as physical and observable impact on the victim, including anxiety, loneliness, headaches, sleep difficulties, low self-esteem, and even depression. It is important to recognise the signs of harassment if you suspect that anyone you know is being harassed. The primary indicator is discomfort and any inappropriate physical, visual, verbal, or emotional contact. If your 'no' has no effect and you are subjected to sexual or unwanted jokes, you are being sexually harassed.

There are many provisions and laws against harassment, such as POSH Law, Sec 503 IPC, and Sec 67 IT Act, but laws cannot bring mental change as changes are needed in the mentality of the individuals living in the society, not only in the form of laws.

As reported by The Economic Times, #MeToo: A survey says nearly 80% of women never report harassment, indicating a flawed redressal system despite the Vishakha Guidelines and the Sexual Harassment of Women at Workplace (Prevention, Prohibition, and Redressal) Act, 2013 enacting rules on the issue. A fundamental condition for implementing any law in the society that benefits women is a change in people's attitudes. Through the act of standing up for the helpless without being judgmental but with empathy, we can strengthen innocent people's willpower to fight for themselves. Justice has the greatest chance of reaching every corner of the earth if laws are appropriately implemented and enforced. We must fight back against the shame associated with our patriarchal society and punish the harasser, not the victim.

CHAPTER SIX

Students, Stress and Substance Abuse

Stress and Substance Abuse:

Stress is the body's reaction to external events, and it can be the outcome of a single incident or ongoing problems. These incidents or problems might be acceptable or undesirable for an individual, such as the beginning of a new school or college, the approach of parents towards their children, financial issues, getting married or divorced, having a baby, being unwell, losing a loved one, relocating, or being in an accident. We experience three types of stress in our day-to-day lives:

- Everyday stress caused by everyday situations
- Stress caused by a sudden unexpected shift or incident
- Stress caused by a traumatic incident

Changes take place in the brain and body when a person is stressed. The heart rate intensifies; pulse rate increases; concentration, attention, and the senses sharpen; and the urge to sleep and eat decreases. Each of us copes with stress differently, and some may turn to inappropriate stress management strategies, such as substance abuse. Stress can raise a person's likelihood of consuming drugs; in fact, stressed individuals are more prone to use mind-altering substances.

Stress is the most well-known contributing factor to drug addiction and relapse susceptibility. Many stressed people drink alcohol or consume drugs to calm themselves every day. So, before we go ahead, ask yourself, Is drinking alcohol or consuming substances beneficial for all of the symptoms of stress? Is it true that consuming drugs increases stress or helps individuals cope with stress?

When stressed, the idea of taking a pill, sedative drugs or a drink and suddenly having the energy to perform more chores in less time may sound enticing, or you might feel calm for a while. People frequently take stimulants, particularly prescription stimulants, to lower their workload or control their anger or stress. One of the most serious issues with the stress-stimulant relationship is the increased possibility of addiction which we ignore most of the time. Nowadays, it is common to consume alcohol or take drugs to ease tension. Despite anecdotal evidence that drinking can help a person relax, using alcohol or drugs to cope with stress is useless. When combined with stress symptoms, the physical side effects of alcohol usage or drugs may wreak havoc on the body. Aside from potential health risks, going to alcohol every time a stressful circumstance arises inhibits the development of natural coping mechanisms.

Students and Substance Abuse:

The factors contributing to the high incidence of drug usage among college students are Curiosity, peer pressure, stress, and course load.

Today's generation tries to explore new aspects of life on their own. It is not unusual for this self-exploration to lead today's young age to drug use. The celebrities we follow on social media largely affect what we want to do in our life. Following idols that are into drugs or seeing videos over the internet and forcing themselves to experiment the same is not uncommon nowadays.

College students accompanied by other students, and friends, who are using pleasure drugs for sleep and performance, are more inclined to trial those drugs themselves. The friend circle with whom we move is the most common cause of drug abuse nowadays. One drug addict involves more people every next day, and the chain is growing on. Parents providing money to their children without even asking for the reason gives it a more push. The easy availability of such drugs is pushing our society to our darker end. Time is not far when we will see drug addicts on the street if strict legal action is not taken at this moment. We as citizens are responsible for the growth of drug abuse, as we see students at places where they should not be or carry stuff they should not be having. The same reason is why theft cases are rising, as the same drug addicts get into a robbery when they don't get enough money from family.

Many students turn to drugs to deal with the intense demands of academics, internships, part-time jobs, social duties, and other obligations. Students nowadays are turning to stimulants like Adderall to make them stay up long enough to work or complete coursework by the due date. These prescription medicines are often acquired without a valid prescription.

These reasons seem to be unclear why a student may experiment with drugs or alcohol. They may be attempting to conceal prior trauma. They might be maintaining a habit that they started in high school. The liberty of being away from family and the easy availability of drugs and alcohol make it easy to explore.

How can we as an individual or society help?

This is the right time for us as an individual or society to reform our strategy for alcohol and drug use disorders before it's too late. Letting our community degrade or upgrade is in our hands. It is precisely the same when we think of ourselves or loved ones whom we want to take pen over drugs. The story doesn't end at our home; keeping a check on your child or your loved ones, you have to help your society in this cause; Holding webinars, seminars and group discussions to make people aware of drug abuse. We find syringes, sedative tablet packets, or cannabis growing in many places nowadays. Either we ignore them, or we don't know what these are. If we know, we should not keep it within ourselves; making our society aware of this evil is our duty. Doctors cannot roam around in graveyards and old buildings or under-construction structures; our responsibility is to check these places. Doctors can help them with a specific medicine or counselling lessons, but we have to check where it comes from, who is helping them, what the cause is, and why the percentage increases. If we find any clue about anyone or any place where this crime occurs, it is better to take help from any professional and perform your duty.

Everyone can understand stress management, but it requires practice. Here are some helpful hints:

Look for yourself: Healthy nutrition, exercise, and adequate sleep can lift your mood and ability to cope! Believe in yourself that you can overcome any difficulty. Each of us experiences ups and downs in life, but that doesn't mean the downs of our life will push us into something from which we can never come out. Drugs are never a solution for stress.

Focus: To avoid getting overwhelmed, take on one task at a time. There is no need to work more than your body isn't comfortable. You can skip your chores if you want to. Give time to yourself, heal up and come back better.

Maintain your cool: Take a deep breath and step away from the argument, fight or conflict. Go for a walk, drive, picnic or do some other form of physical activity. There is no need to get into an argument which will degrade your mental health. Learn how to forgive and forget; that will help you to become a better person.

Continue your journey: If you don't succeed the first time, practise and prepare for another time. Alternatively, you might participate in another activity. Failure doesn't mean the end; it is just a part of life. No one is perfect; we all face failures, which makes us perfect.

Let's talk about it: Speaking with an empathetic listener who keeps calm may be beneficial. If you are stressed, talk to a close friend, or you can visit a psychologist or counsellor for the same. But if you opt for drugs over a talk, it is going to affect you and push you to end your life in the long run. No matter what, your parents, teachers, friends and siblings can be the best listeners; you need to approach the right person according to the situation.

CHAPTER SEVEN

Invigilation and Academic Dishonesty

EXAMINATION INVIGILATOR:

An exam invigilator is a person employed by the board of examination to ensure the effective conduct of an examination following proper rules and regulations. The exam invigilator is responsible for monitoring the applicants or students to prevent fraudulent activities during the examination. They must ensure that all examinations follow the rules established by the examination board, allowing each applicant to sit for the test under the same conditions as other candidates across the country.

INVIGILATORS WAY OF CONDUCT:

How an invigilator progresses inside the examination hall significantly impacts how students sit for the next 3 hours of the examination. It is not that an invigilator should laugh and start cracking jokes, but they also cannot stress students before the test with their behavior. If he starts discussing his success stories and warning students about the next 3 hours, it will worry students more, leading to poor performance. The priority should always be something motivational that can help students build their positive mindset for the next three hours; checking the palm and arms of students, pouch, cardboard, pockets, and wallets should always be the second priority for an invigilator. If an invigilator cannot motivate their students in the examination hall, they have no right to demotivate them. Shouting at a student trying to copy-paste from the successive student has the worst impact on other students who try to focus on their Paper. Examination halls are more like the day of judgment as if we are sitting in front of God, and if we lie, we will be pushed into the hellfire; hardly a few invigilators try to maintain a stress-free environment in the examination hall. Most of us have witnessed the examination hall's atmosphere and invigilators' different mindsets. I have experienced that some of the invigilators are there to give students free stress out of nowhere.

MY EXPERIENCE AS AN APPLICANT SITTING IN THE EXAMINATION HALL:

Since Day 1 of my school, I was taught exam is what you know. Your result will show where you are, so in simple language, my exams are going to decide my intelligence, my hard work, my capabilities, my dedication, my potential, my ability, and my results are going to determine my future. But sorry, I disagree, I am a writer, and I do not need integration in my write-ups.

I have failed to write in some of my papers; even though I had prepared what I was supposed to, I still couldn't write up to my expectations. So, whenever I sat in the examination hall, I was stressed more because of the invigilator than my question paper. Being a student, I would like to share some suggestions for invigilators to support stressed applicants:

Examiners must be aware that where a student sits can significantly impact how they feel in the examination room and that applicants can be moved if necessary.

Examiners should try to listen to applicants calmly if they have any issues; shouting at them without knowing adds to a stressed applicant.

REASONS BEHIND ACADEMIC DISHONESTY:

Students' inability to balance the demands of their academic and social lives is one of the most prevalent reasons for academic dishonesty. Students who struggle to organize their workload and other commitments often fall behind on their deadlines and turn to dishonesty as a quick fix.

Some students accuse their teachers of being too demanding or difficult to comprehend, which they claim is the cause of their dishonesty. Additionally, students may argue that a course was inappropriate for their major or that the exams were unfair. Sometimes students believe that because other students are cheating, they have no choice but to do the same.

Some students may cheat in exams due to anxiety over their academic achievement. Students who want to pass a class or get good grades may engage in academic dishonesty. Some students may use cheating to cope with their subpar test-taking abilities.

Students can compel other students into academic cheating in several ways, including by pressuring them to collaborate during exams or by helping them outside the exam hall, by witnessing other pupils cheat and then joining them, by engaging in academic cheating in groups, and by assisting friends during exams.

"WHEN I WAS CAUGHT BLUE HANDED":

This incident took place back in 2012 when I was in 7th grade. We all are aware of the uneasy calm that prevails in Kashmir and the most affected sector is the education sector.

In 2012, the situation was very tense in state Jammu and Kashmir. All Educational institutions remained closed for about 6 months. I had just stepped into teenage, the age where enjoying life is the first priority than focusing on the goals of your life. While enjoying my holidays, we all received a shocking news that the date sheet for our final exams was released. Nobody was mentally prepared for appearing in the exams. Everything was out of my mind; no touch with books for 6 months. I knew nothing, I had even forgotten how to read and write. Everything seemed to be so puzzling. After wasting all days with what to prepare, how to prepare, and where to start from, the day of the final exams arrived. I wasted the whole night praying to God that "Please! Cancel these exams; I will study from the beginning in the next standard." But finally, I got ready for school and when I boarded the school bus with a sad face and already thinking about the outcome of my paper, I noticed that nobody else was worried about the exam, it was just a normal day for them. I thought to myself, "Am I living in a dream or is the paper cancelled?" I sat on my seat, opened my book to grasp some last-minute knowledge, but all in vain.

Finally, I asked one of my classmates that how he is sitting so comfortably without even opening the book. He and my other classmates who were sitting next to him showed me their hands filled with 50% of the syllabus. I was shocked to see this and at the same time pitying my innocence that how could I not think of such a plan. They insisted me; "If you want to save yourself from the taunt of your parents, fill your hand before we reach the school." I never thought of the consequences, without wasting any time, I went rushing to the back seat, opened my book, took out my blue gel pen (which was supposed to fill my answer sheet first, but unfortunately was filling my hand). Everyone had written on the inner side of the hand, but I was really inexperienced and in the heat of the moment, I wrote on the upper side of my hand. You might be thinking that how can I be so careless, but no, I was just trying to be 2 steps forward than the others, I thought I will write everything on my hand and for sure the question paper will have these questions.

When we reached school after a long break of 6 months, we rushed in search of our examination rooms and sat on our allotted seats. I was so happy, that I will do great in today's paper, and I thought now I don't need to study a word in this class as I have an amazing technique for the rest of the papers too. Just when the question paper and answer sheets were dropped on our table, I had butterflies in my stomach seeing that more than 80% of the question paper was written on my hand.

Everyone started copy pasting, either from their mind or hands, I was taking the help of my hand instead of my mind. I was sitting on the 4th row, and the teacher who was on duty caught me while signing my answer sheet. You can't say he caught me red-handed because my hands were blue! He caught me blue-handed. I was just shocked that I was caught at the last moment of the first paper. He had turned all red with anger and asked me that what is this? I was quiet for a while, clenching my fists and thinking of any excuse that could come to my mind. After a few seconds, Sir was angrier and asked with a hoarse voice "What is this? Should I take you to the Principal's office?" I tried to be innocent and possibly gave the lamest excuse that I was just practicing my answers. With a horrifying voice, Sir asked, "Didn't you have a notebook or a sheet of paper?"

and while uttering these words, he snatched my paper. I was trying to be as serious as possible, but while all this was happening, all the other cheaters were spitting on their hands and erasing all the evidence that they are cheating too.

When I left the examination hall, all my classmates came to me and asked, "Why had you written on the upper side of your hand?" I felt the ground slipping under my feet and with a shaky voice, I asked them, "Will sir call my parents?" (As he had taken pictures of my hand). Obviously, he told my parents about it, and although around 7 years have passed since this incident, I still get teased by my family members and we laugh it off that how could I write on the top of my hand. Guess I didn't have much akal then. How true is it, "nakal karne kay liay bhi akal honi chahiyay".

Virtual Classes – A Bane For Student Community

"A major contribution to the poor mental health of students since the beginning of the pandemic"

Unfortunately, when the pandemic hit globally no one knew until when it would continue. Countries across the globe chose 'Lockdown' as the only way to contain the further spread of the deadly infection. However, the cases kept on swelling with each day as of 2 August 2021, there have been 198,022,041 confirmed cases of COVID-19, including 4,223,460 deaths, reported to WHO.

During this pandemic people lost their lives, jobs, social life, family, and a majority of people wasted their time without their will. This concern rose, so the future of students was at stake too, since all educational institutions were closed for in-campus classes. Authorities decided to go for online classes via platforms including Zoom, Skype, WebEx, Google Meet, etc and nobody knows till when this will continue. It has been around 16 months that the classes are being taken virtually.

Firstly, isn't it difficult for a student to manage 6 hours of online classes and doing basic household chores? Keeping a phone in one hand and doing household chores with the other was never a concern for his/her parents or teaching staff. It's obvious that the classwork won't stop for one student, so he/she has to manage it all together.

Secondly, students not having access to android phones, and a good internet connection; has anyone approached them? No! They are left depressed with what's actually going on in these virtual classes, as they have no way to attend this unconventional medium. Every time they fail to attend classes, get their assignments submitted, and are left with zero percent attendance, and are supposed to borrow a phone or even an internet connection to appear in online exams. However, with nobody batting an eye towards them, has left these poor souls with no choice, other than just waiting for this pandemic to end.

One of the major concerns in virtual classes is turning on your camera and microphone. When the teacher suddenly asks a student to turn on his/her camera and microphone, it isn't as easy as it seems to be, you have to be ready to face criticism, it's obvious you feel uglier than others, having messy hair, sleepy eyes, showing your personal space. It is obvious and understandable that we all are afraid of being judged by our physical appearance, afraid of falling to those "bullies" who capture screenshots and then these screenshots revolve in the class groups, being teased, is what adds more to the deterioration of the already ailing student community from the average or below average families. It is not easy for anyone to come up like this in a virtual world. At times, when a teacher asks you a question and you are speechless, with no appropriate answer, meanwhile thinking what others are thinking about you right now.

While being in a virtual class, you are supposed to be alone in your room to stay more focused. Being alone in a room for repetitive classes, we start feeling bad about the static life we've been surviving in, since the beginning of this pandemic. One class ends and others are already in the queue. It's obvious that when you are alone, you think more and this is what leads to silent depression with no one to listen to your worries.

Apart from all of this, the students are already having a hard time attending online classes, making notes, submitting assignments, maintaining attendance, waiting for a date sheet with no other curricular activities with seminars and conferences turning to webinars with no outdoor activity, all the stuff students used to do outdoors have been restricted to a "Smartphone". How is it possible that any student will be comfortable with it? Humans are termed as social animals and socializing is a very important part of our lives, but unfortunately, we all are focused on the rising COVID-19 cases but not the mental health of students.

Adding one more concern to the list is that, Is it possible for a student to understand cent percent of the topic in a virtual class? The e-books were introduced to save paper, but these virtual classes aren't able to save our education. Students hardly understand 50% of what is being taught because of which students fail to get a good percentage (of marks, as well as understanding). And we all are well aware of how parents are obsessed with the mark's percentage of their wards. Also, in this competitive world when you get low grades, you lose many opportunities in your future which in turn will add more to the mental disturbance of a student.

And last but not the least, using a phone for 6 hours to attend virtual classes and then making notes from the same phone for another 4-6 hours with no rest in between, isn't possible for a normal human being. If anyone is given a cell phone for 12 hours, it won't make him/her feel better in any way. It's obvious that in the long run, it's going to affect our eyes and in turn, it is going to make us unhealthy.

Some of the known cases of suicide, linked to the online mode of teaching have been mentioned below. But it's really unfortunate that they were not highlighted like any other suicide cases. According to a news article reported by India Today (Akshaya Nath), a class 11 student from Tamil Nadu ended his life, after failing to cope up with the pressure of online classes, one more girl from the same state ended her life after getting into an argument over sharing the mobile phone with her sisters for virtual classes and in June, a 12-year-old schoolgirl from Gujarat's Rajkot died by committing suicide after being frustrated with online classes and homework - her father had recently bought her a Smartphone for the online classes after much struggle. There are many cases like this; some of them just came on social media for a day or two, and others were just dumped. I saw no one raising a voice against it, no one talking about it, no one showing any sort of concern regarding it, and obviously, no action seems in sight to find alternative ways of "socializing" and getting an education.

In the end, I leave a question for all the readers out there are these so-called "smartphones" sharing their smartness with us? Or are they turning us into a slave of "tech giants", hence making us dumber and more dependable on them? Will wait for a response from the learned readers.

CHAPTER NINE

The Discriminated Aging

"Don't rely on anyone else to accomplish your goals; you have to do it, make it happen, and achieve it.
Mohmod Irfan Shah *"*

It is not wrong to say that aging is a different experience for different classes of our society. However, intense stress induces premature aging, and the level of stress largely depends on various factors such as physical health, the quality of our relationship, promises, responsibilities, and the degree to which we depend and expect from others.

In every class of our society, we will see no age group without mental stress, ending with premature aging. It all starts when you are born, you are taught to compete with people around you till you are no more a participant in this world.

The first step outside our home is schooling, getting admission to a school with all types of facilities and co-curricular activities. Children from high-class (higher income) societies get admission in leading private schools while subsistence society (lower income) opt for

Government schools. They get free education with middeal meals according to their financial status. Getting admission to a top school is the first challenge for burgherdom society (middle-income group). There is a paradox as to which school should they opt for; opting for a government school will safeguard their savings for other expenses like construction or renovation of the house, buying a new car, setting up a business while opting for a top private school will assure their child's career up to some extent. These children are not mature enough to decide what their aim in life is; their mind has not grown enough to determine their will. Children are forced within the four walls of a school building, even if they are interested, to go to the playground, drawing, writing or being creative by discovering new things.

Here comes the next stage of life, which is the most crucial, when the child enters the age of adolescence, where they have to face the real world, where they will come across different ups and downs, where they have to deal with good and evil on their own and have to face day-to-day bullies. Most high-class children choose friends of their status, while other children prefer to stay around people they can fit in with. Burgherdom class children (middle-income group) face different problems; choosing a friend from a High-Class society might induce an inferiority complex. Eventually, they will get stressed about their lives and become ungrateful by complaining too much about their lives. If they choose a friend from the Subsistence class (Below the poverty line), it stresses them with their friend's condition and makes them feel sorry for the discrimination based on earnings.

Crossing the teenage, the same child enters the competitive world, where all the children from different classes want to get admission in top courses in well-ranked colleges. At this stage, if children from High-class society fail to get admission in Top Government colleges, their parents are ready to get admission in Leading Private Colleges for their children, and for children from subsistence society (below the poverty line) either get a seat in Government Colleges with the help of a reserved quota for them by the Government or get a scholarship for their admission in any undergraduate course. In contrast, children from Burgherdom society (middle income group) get into a do or die situation; either they have to work hard to gain admission to Government College, or their parents have to pressurize them to choose any college which is just a compromise on their part. In the end, this child either ends up in a degree college for graduation in any stream even if they are capable of being a sound doctor/Engineer/ Professor, or they have to see their parents spending their lifetime earnings on them, which makes them feel sorry for the whole upcoming life.

In the next stage of their lives, students are stressed as they have to make sure that they get a degree with a high percentage, but what stresses them more is finding a job so that they are well settled and independent. At this stage, children from High-class society are not tensed because either their ancestors already own a business or their ménage set up a new business for them. On the other hand, Subsistence class children (Low-income group) have either worked very hard and gotten placed hence found a way out to earn their livelihood. However, if they fail to get a job, they are forced to opt for other jobs, be it farming, working as a salesman, or working as a domestic help in high-class society homes. Again, students from Burgherdom class (middle-income group) are left with no option if they fail to get a good government job or in any private sector. Most of the time, they do not own a family business or cannot set up a new one; they get offended working as laborers, farmers, or sales assistants. They stress themselves with their situation and blame themselves, their family, and their existence, resulting in them getting depressed.

The final stage of this stressful life is to get married to a well-off family. In this case, too, high-class society parents get their children quickly married without asking for a degree, job, and background. Subsistence society (lower income group) finds someone of their status, matching the family background same income, lifestyle, etc. Here, in Burgherdom society (middle-income group), if they want to get married to a well-off family, they should be of the same standard. If they choose to marry someone from the Subsistence class, they do not feel comfortable doing so as society looks down on such people.

Therefore, we can say that the people of burgherdom and subsistence class have it difficult. They need to push themselves up and burn the midnight oil to make ends meet. It is true that hard work and smart work matter, but luck also plays a significant role in our lives.

A SHORT STORY BASED ON TRUE EVENT

This incident took place back in the year 2019, on the 20th of April.

Do you know how most people deal with their life? Not everyone here is a Government employee or in a high-class private sector. High-income or middle-income group families are okay with their lifestyle; they earn, spend, and save some of it for future expenditures; be it family trips, family functions, or teaching their children in leading private colleges. Think of those who earn some bucks, be it by working in a workshop, working as a maid, selling newspapers in streets or begging in full daylight and then buying something to eat for the night, for their whole family. They earn and spend, and no savings at all.

On that very day, I saw a boy, who will not be more than 15, I guess, he worked in a car washing station, worked hard to earn some money and maybe had a large family behind. Lol! Child labour is banned in India. Who cares for this class? Who cares for his future? Who will manage his family if he won't work hard?

I was standing behind him, and meanwhile, his boss came, you know what he said to him? Ahh, it was heart-breaking; with a murmuring voice, he said, "Bas, yi cha last-ich gaed" (This is the last car for today), and his boss replied, "Bas chuni aasaan" (there is no end to anything). What would he do? He just kept going on, didn't care what the time was, how much was left. It was almost 6:30, and he was still working, maybe praying to Allah that no Cars come after this so that he could go home early.

Do you know why did I drop this story? So that you and I realise what people go through, how lucky we are, how fortunate we are that we have every kind of facility. Just think, if we were in his place, what would we do? Allah has blessed us with everything we need. So work hard to achieve what you want. Don't rely on anyone else; you have to do it, make it, and automatically achieve it.

It's well said by Calvin Coolidge that "All growth depends upon activity. There is no development physically or intellectually without effort, and effort means work."

CHAPTER TEN

"Marriage – Commitment Or A Business Deal?"

Nikaah ceremonies of different couples were going on in other rooms of a marriage hall. The building was built to hold social gatherings for many people, with more investment in purposeless stuff. I watched everything from the back of the door as I was waiting for one of my relatives' Nikaah ceremony to start. I could see no one with an average T-Shirt and Pant; everyone was wearing a tight nice branded suit. It was so confusing to differentiate between bride-groom and function attendees, almost everyone wearing a Raymond Suit and Rolex watch; I glanced at my Casio digital watch to see if it is still showing the same time as it is used to before.

While roaming around, my eyes caught a scene from outside, and I was shocked to witness an incident where workers were throwing the remaining food away, with beggars not allowed to enter the ceremonies of these royal men. I just ran to them and asked that why they were throwing away so much food? They replied that this was the leftover and extra food. I just told them, kindly pour as much as they can eat, not less, not more, to this they replied that the bride's father has said pour more, so that Grooms family doesn't feel, they are miser! To this. I thought to myself how unfortunate I am to witness such moments and what we have emerged to as a society? If one tries to save food, people will label you as a "Miser."

I left from there and went downstairs to go to the washroom, and I saw my relatives, headed by Groom's father, who was talking so furiously, confused about the following steps to go ahead. Just when we came upstairs in the corridor, we were welcomed by the host. We were given room 919 and told to follow the group of men who would be assisting us. When we were near room 918, the Nikaah ceremony of one of our faraway relatives was also going on. I could see a beautiful carpet with a beautiful stage, and table and chairs with dry fruit bowls and drinks, and much more over the table. One of my uncles went to them for casual greetings. On turning back, his eye caught the dry fruit bowls having 500's, and 2000's Gandhi Ji notes; he went there and picked one note and some dry fruits and left. Instead of being astonished that he took the money from there, I was more puzzled that such a considerable amount of money was kept in mere dry fruit bowls, with no apparent motive. All of us picked some money and dry fruits, including me, from those beautiful copper bowls and passed a smile to that family.

Once we left, we were just a few steps away from room 919; I ran back towards room 918 and kept that money back in the dry fruit bowl. On seeing this, someone enquired why I kept that money back in the bowl, to this I replied; does it belong to you? He said; No, but it is for people around here. I replied, that what is the purpose of keeping money for people? Are the attendee's poor?

To this, everyone stared at me with evil eyes, as If I had committed a sin or said something against their religion.

The bride's father replied: It's a rule now; to invest all the money you have saved for your whole life on your daughter's marriage, to fulfil the demands of the groom's family, to ensure they are not left empty. It is a way of respecting the Grooms family as they are being given all the possible privileges on this day because their son is getting married to our daughter. On listening to the tone of his voice, I felt as if his daughter was a burden on him.

I was shocked to hear his stammering voice while saying so; I went to his daughter and said, "How can you accept this marriage when you are being treated like a business deal? I hope you care about how your father has earned and invested it for his daughter to get accepted. "

To this, some men came and thrashed me away from the room. I ran downstairs to the reception desk to check the files of both bride and groom. I was again shocked with what I found that the bride has done Masters in Science and was a private school teacher while as the groom wasn't even much educated. To accept the marriage proposal, there was a deal that her father has to set up a shop for Groom, and 30 lakh cash for the renovation of the house and a car not worth less than 8 lakh and some jewellery and dresses for Grooms relatives.

I ran back to the room and shouted at the groom's father, "Wish you had taught your son, today he would have been a sober/prudent guy, not demanding, but accepting the sacrifice of the bride's father who is giving his daughter forever." I recalled the scene when my family members were taking money from those dry fruit boxes in a straight line, one followed by the other; only I came back, nobody else even tried. Same like that, the meaningless traditions of our society will never end until one takes a U-Turn at a personal level, and I am sure people will follow that because no one uses his mind to decide what is right and what is wrong. Society runs in a straight path; if one person turns their back on such nonsensical things, others will surely follow him.

All the people in the building gathered; my relatives came and dropped the money in the dry fruit bowls. Everyone started appreciating me for stating the obvious facts about the traditions which should never have been practiced.

It was reported by a non-governmental organization (NGO) in April 2021 that around 50 thousand Kashmiri females are still unmarried despite having reached the marriageable age of 18. Unnecessary customs and rituals are to blame for the valley's late marriage epidemic. Aside from financial restrictions and dowry expectations, competitiveness in give-take procedures is also a contributing factor to delayed marriages.

It is worth appreciation that in Badaghar Babe Wayil village of Ganderbal, all the villagers have signed a stamp paper pledging that they would neither accept nor offer dowry. Simple weddings have been a part of this village's culture for more than 30 years. Hence, we all should follow their footsteps and ponder over the fact whether a marriage is a business deal or a lifetime commitment?

(This is a fictional piece of writing by Mohmod Irfan Shah, All of the characters, businesses, locations, events or incidents described in this article are either the product of the author's imagination or have been created in a fictitious manner. The sole purpose of the write-up is to open the eyes of people who have been blinded by show-off and to guide them in opening

their eyes and make them understand that how the act of an individual results in putting unbearable pressure upon the masses.)

• 49 •

Is 'New Year' a theme for change?

"*A fresh beginning may occur on any day of the year if you make the decision to start anything new.*
Mohmod Irfan Shah"

The beginning of a new calendar year or adding up of the calendar years count by one is marked by New Year's Eve celebration. Different cultures celebrate the occasion in different ways across the whole world. The month of January is considered to be the worldwide or conventional start of the civil year. New Year eve is no less than a religious festival in today's era. People mark it as a holiday to forget the sorrows of the previous year and welcome the happiness of the upcoming one, forgetting that one more precious year of their life has ended.

For many people, the Common theme of New Year is that, December 31st is a time to look back on the last 12 months and reflect on how we've progressed and what we've accomplished. They celebrate the changes and trials that they have overcome, and they think this is the moment to do so and celebrate their survival.

The beginning of a new year is a time for introspection and consideration of possibilities, so it doesn't matter whether you celebrate or party at the end. Most of us recapitulate, take out some time for ourselves to think about what we did in the last year, which affected our mental, physical and social life and come up with a positive approach for the upcoming year. But from my personal experience, by evaluating yourself at the end of the year, there are least chances that you are going to be better in any way; better is to give yourself some time and try to build a positive change in yourself at any time of the year.

Predicting the upcoming year will come up with a success story for you to forget the downs of life. There is no assurance that you will achieve whatever you have pointed for your upcoming year. Better is to get ready for the forthcoming failures and keep a firm belief that you will surpass them with confidence.

There is no proof of overnight success since the beginning of the calendar. So, it's better to make an effort to be optimistic while remaining realistic. Make a plan, but be prepared to change course if the situation changes to the downward side. On never year Eve, while at a party or some function it's definite, you'll have plenty of company when you're attempting to make positive changes in your life, but you forget at the end you will have to go back home alone, face alone and tackle alone whatever is going to come up in the coming year.

On New Year's Eve, there's nothing better than toasting to the fact that we've survived another year of life's turmoil that too in this pandemic where we lost many of our loved ones. In many ways, the trials of the past two years have been beyond distressing; either people lost their job, or their loved ones or their dedication towards work. Many of us had kept some goals for these two years, but few people succeeded. And we still are surviving in the pandemic, so let's be positive, confident and ready to tackle.

New Year's resolutions are set by people all over the globe every year in order to achieve their goals, improve their overall health, and generally make their lives better. Many people succeed in following their New Year's resolutions, but many others fail to do so.

According to a Discover Happy Habits survey, 75% of people who make New Year's resolutions keep them after a week. After two weeks, it reduces to 71%. After a month, the number lowers to 64%. And six months later, 46% of those who set resolutions still keep them. After six months, only 4% of people who have similar goals but do not make a resolution still succeed.

Beginnings and changes in our lives are sparked by the start of a new year; however, that spark should last throughout the year rather than fizzle out after a few days or weeks. Instead of making emotional resolutions that you may later realise to be impracticable or uninteresting, you should learn to make practical resolutions that are based on common sense and facts rather than on emotion.

A fresh beginning may occur on any day of the year if you make the decision to start anything new. Although a new year does not immediately transform us or our attitude on life, it may serve as a natural beginning point for altering our thoughts and actions.

CHAPTER TWELVE

Are you donating or fueling the scam?

Not all people in this world come with the privilege to be born in a wealthy family, even if our ancestors didn't have a luxurious lifestyle, but we can create one for us and our coming generations. After coming into this world, everyone is not lucky enough to be someone from a financially stable family. We either can work hard and make our living style better or do nothing to change our lifestyle. God made us all, with different faces but the same mind. Yes, it's scientifically proven that the intelligence level of the brain is not the same, the intelligence varies from person to person, but the hard and smart work depends on you, we can earn in a halaal way to make our lives better instead of begging or stealing. We can work hard today for a better life tomorrow.

Indeed in our society, there are people with different financial conditions, so it becomes a responsibility for people with good financial conditions to help poor people in their vicinity or neighborhood. We can help people by donating clothes, money, offering them work, or providing them with food and shelter. We can donate money to poor people so that they can live their life in a better way.

A question worth pondering: If we have entrepreneurs like Jeff Bezos, Elon Musk, and Bill Gates in the world, why don't they donate a huge portion of their property among people and eradicate poverty?

Yes, definitely such personalities can eradicate poverty, but they don't do it. Because if they do so, no one will work, and they will keep waiting for the donations, and this will, in turn, stop development and the competition in this world.

Begging or Begging scams?

People in our society have gotten used to asking money, except those who genuinely need it; we see healthy people with good conditions to work begging outside religious spots, roads, educational institutions, traffic signals, or coming directly to our home. We keep donating in Allah's way, but we fail to reach people who don't come out to beg or don't come up to ask for help and the ones who might genuinely need financial assistance. Begging has become a way to earn money without effort, and it's becoming the next emerging evil of our society.

Do you verify the case before donating?

Every next day we find donation requests on social media; not every request is genuine or verified. We blindly keep transferring money into their accounts with our good intentions to help them overcome their problem, and in a couple of days or in most cases within hours, the account gets a donation of lakhs of rupees. The donation requests vary from a person who doesn't have a roof to live under or someone who has been abandoned by family to someone who doesn't have enough amount of money to fight a deadly disease. If the said person is in need of 10lakh rupees s/he gets double or triple times more than that within no time.

But, have we ever left our homes to check upon our neighbour? Maybe there are people around in our neighbourhood who can't even afford meals; we forget people who are differently-abled, we forget widows and orphans, as we keep donating via online platform thinking we are doing it for our akhirah, indeed we are doing it for our own good, but we hardly verify the case on our own, we hardly try to check how much has already been transferred, or is the money even going to the right person.

I am not against donations over an online platform, but can't we replace this trend with a way through which the needy person gets what they actually need? Filling one account with more than what they actually need and leaving 100's of others hungry won't bring justice to people who even after burning the midnight oil are hardly making the ends meet.

The problem that has been presented before you in the previous paragraph might not seem to be of huge scale. But, once we start thinking about it, one will come to realise that if the money keeps getting transferred even after the required amount is donated to the person's account, it becomes kind of a scam. And this happens due to various reasons. Our social media apps do not sort the feed/ posts on the basis of time, the algorithm of various social media platforms is different; in simpler terms, if a donation request might have been uploaded by a person/ page on a particular day there is a high probability that it will pop up on your feed even after the required amount is donated and because of this, very often, the donation amount exceeds the required amount.

After thinking about possible solutions to this problem, here are a few suggestions from my end:

Firstly, it is the responsibility of people who promote such requests to keep a check on the donations and as soon as the donation request is met, the previous request must be removed from all social media sites and replaced by a post saying "The donation request has been completed."

Secondly, a number of places already have area wise Bayt al-mal for the people in need, other than that, a number of NGOs are present in our valley. We can constantly promote such organizations and ask people to make donations as per their wish. Therefore, if a need arises, the people in need can verify their details and their case at the Bayt al-mal or NGO and hence the desired amount can be transferred to their account. Also, a GoFundMe like website can be developed in which the donation request automatically closes after the required amount is met.

We must prefer hiring people who are in good health after verifying their background and personal detail which will stopping them from begging. Collecting money for building religious places, asking money from people on road for shrines or spending money ruthlessly for nazroniyaaz in ziyarats, Masjids or Temples won't fix the emerging evils and increasing poverty of our society.

Unfortunately, a significant amount of begging is carried out by organised criminals. When you contribute to beggars, you have no way of knowing if you are assisting them or just fueling the criminal ring. Therefore, we must unite for the cause of helping people overcome their financial problems while also taking care of the fact that we do not fuel the crime ring.

CHAPTER THIRTEEN

Getting over it: How do we overcome the fear of moving on?

"You exist, even after failing, is the positive attitude you should hold onto."
Mohmod Irfan Shah. *"*

So, let me explain it to you.

I know many of us are going through this, be it a girl left by her boyfriend or a boy left by his girlfriend, husband divorced by his wife or wife divorced by her husband, or old parents left by their children. So, it is obvious that you will feel anxious after something like this has happened with you. The thing that actually makes us anxious is the fact that the person leaving will no more be with you, s/he will not celebrate your joy, will not lift you when you are in sorrow, will not be with you anymore.

For me, there are, three sides of mindset. For example, a man who is married and has kids, at the minimum has three ways to treat people, with his wife he will behave in a particular manner, with his children in a different manner and he will have different behaviour towards his parents as well.

As a son, he is born on the very first day of his life, as a husband, he is born again on the day of his marriage, and finally, as a father, he is born when he has a child. So, when he has to interact with them, be it his parents, his wife, his child, his behaviour, his thoughts, his feelings, his plans for future, his attachment changes in each case. His thoughts as a father are different from what they are as his parent's son or his wife's husband. When he sees or listens to his father his behaviour of being a son activates, when he sees/listens to his wife his behaviour of being a husband activates, when he sees/listens to his child, his behaviour of being a father activates. These three feelings and ways of responding to each are different.

Noted? These three aspects of a man's life make three different persons. His thoughts, his body language, his way of talking is different in every case.

Now, if this man gets a divorce from his wife, so one of his character as a husband, to play, is over, he is no more a husband now but there are still two roles, in him, to play. A father and a son is still there. But if you think positively and differently, you will realise that one who got divorced from his wife is sad, but the other two i.e., son and father are still happy, are still the same. Now he

is no more a husband. Now an another new person will come into existence that is, an ex-husband, because his thoughts and feelings are too different from the husband he had been with before he got the divorce. You have to realise it, that the husband in him has died now, he has to focus on the other two beings in him, "father and son".

Even if all the persons stop existing at any moment of your life, it should not affect you in any way.

You as a father, can die, you as a son, can die, you as a husband, as a brother, as a friend, as an employee, can die, everything has an end to it. But we know, one of the roles in a person's life that dies or does not exist anymore does not make the person dead as a whole, because he has the capability of performing any other role in his life.

You gave birth to yourself as a father and a husband, If the husband is no more, he is still capable of performing all other roles in his life.

Even if you don't want to make the husband exist again, you are short of money or situation isn't allowing it, give birth to a new role, become an employee, earn some bucks then do whatever you want to. You are an educated human being, so you can earn easily.

Power is in your hands, choose any of the roles you want to play, you are the director, producer, the actor whose act/ story can flop but is still capable to produce different roles.

It's because of your body, your soul, who can come out in any form and can perform best, God forbid, if you harm yourself or kill yourself, you will not be able to be in any other role.

It all depends on you, how you react, how you take things so it's better to save your life and come in different roles.

And if you be in these roles with a smiling face even after the divorce, a failure, abandonment by a friend, don't let any of them affect you, this is what is called ego. You exist even after failing is the positive ego you should hold onto.